# The Story of TEA

# The Story of TEA

T. Damu

Rupa & Co

Copyright © T. Damu. 2003

Published 2003 by

*Rupa & Co.*
7/16, Ansari Road, Daryaganj,
New Delhi 110 002


Sales Centres:

Allahabad Bangalore Chandigarh Chennai
Dehradun Hyderabad Jaipur Kathmandu
Kolkata Ludhiana Mumbai Pune

All rights reserved.
No part of this publication may be reproduced,
stored in a retrieval system, or transmitted,
in any form or by any means, electronic,
mechanical, photocopying, recording or otherwise,
without the prior permission of the publishers.


Designed by
Proservices Network Pvt. Ltd.
92, Uday Park
New Delhi 110 049

Printed in India by
International Print-O-Pac Ltd.,
B-204, 205, 206 Okhla Industrial Area,
Phase-I, New Delhi-110 020

# Contents

| | |
|---|---|
| The Legend and Origin | 2 |
| The Tea Family | 9 |
| Tea and China | 11 |
| Tea in India | 15 |
| The Global Flow | 24 |
| Boston Tea Party | 35 |
| Changing Trends | 39 |
| Varietieas | 46 |
| Tea Consumption in India | 49 |
| Tea Plantations and Environment | 52 |
| Let Legendary Tea Survive | 58 |
| Tea Varieties | 60 |
| Glossary | 62 |

Tea is a legend. It has always been a dear subject for innumerable researchers. The bibliography on tea runs into massive volumes with stories, treatises, studies and collections. It is not a light subject that could be brewed in a few minutes and poured into a tea cup to sip relaxingly, but one that is oceanous with unfathomable depths.

The plant, whose juice warms many a million hearts around the world and runs as the life line for many and has become an indispensable part of our lives. To know all about tea is fascinating.

# The Legend and Origin

Emperor Shen Nung, one of the three revered mythical emperors of China, belonging to 2737 BC, is believed to be the discoverer of tea. The emperor was well aware of the virtues of boiling water before drinking, and one day while doing so, saw it turn a little brighter and take on a unique flavour when a few leaves from the branches of a nearby tree fell into the kettle. This Divine Healer, to whom the Chinese ascribe much of their botanical knowledge and agro-practices, at once realised the exhilarating and therapeutic values of the magic leaves. This is how, tea was discovered.

But a Japanese legend ascribes the origin of tea to an Indian hermit called Bodhidharma (or Daruma as he is known in Japan). He was the 28th Buddhists' patriarch and the founder of the Dhyan or Zen sect of Buddhism. He is believed to have travelled from India to China in around 526 BC. The then Emperor of China allotted the saint a cave temple for unperturbed meditation for nine years. The avowed ascetic however fell asleep during meditation and on awakening he was so enraged at his own faux pas that he tore of his tired eye-lids and threw them away in disgust. And lo! A strange plant sprouted from the castaway eyelids, which possessed the unique property to drive away sleep and sluggishness!

*A strange plant sprouted from the castaway eyelids*

An Irish-Greek writer, Lafcadio Hearn, in his work 'Some Chinese Ghosts' (1887) wrote that Daruma spoke of the tea plant that had sprung from his plucked eyelids thus: "verily for all time to come, men who drink of thysap shall find such refreshment that wariness may not overcome them nor languor seize upon them—neither shall they know the confusion of drowsiness, nor any desire for slumber in the hour of duty or of prayer. Blessed be thou!"

A less fabulous version of the legend states that when Daruma felt drowsy during meditation he chewed the leaves of a nearby plant and felt invigorated. This legend however is dated 542 AD—much later than the actual use of tea as a beverage in China began.

Yet another Chinese legend gives a totally different but very interesting story: There lived a herbalist, who possessed the wealth of knowledge of 84,000 medicinal herbs. Before his last days, he could acquaint his progency with only 62,000 plants. The secrecy of the remaining herbs seems to have been buried with the deceased. But a miracle happened and wonderful plant grew upon his grave, which was found to possess in itself the virtues of all the lost 22,000 plants! This plant was tea, which by then curing a chronic illness of a court minister's daughter became a plant with lasting fame.

One more Chinese legend tells us that Gan Lu, a Buddhist monk of China came to India in 1st century AD for Buddhist studies and returned with seven tea plants which he planted on Meng mountain in Szechwan.

Though all these legends might make us believe that China is the original home of tea plant, there is still some simmering controversy over this claim. Some scientists as well as historians are not in favour of giving credit to China. The dispute over the proto type from which 3 tea species— namely *Camellia sinensis*, *Camellia assamica* and *Camellia combodiensis* evolved is still not settled. Wild tea bushes discovered in 19th century along the Assam, Manipur, Mizoram, Burma, Thailand, Vietnam and Laos stretch raised a vital question: are they wild or remnants of tea plantations maintained by aboriginal migratory tribes?

Some botanists consider that the first harvest of the leaf of "Miang" or wild tea tree could have been done in these above countries rather than in proper China. The aboriginal tribes beyond southwestern borders of China are still using tea leaves for chewing and for preparing a medicinal beverage from time immemorial. The custom of eating pickled wild tea leaves still prevails among some mountainous tribes of South East Asia. The Singpho and

Khamti tribes of northeast India also have been drinking a tea brew for ages. And with the legends of Gan Lu and Bodhidharma, a school of thought argues in favour of India being the original home of tea.

It is most surprising to note that some Sanskrit scholars in India are of the opinion that *Sanjeevani* plant which finds expression in *Ramayana* may well be tea! Assamese medical scripture *Nidana*, written in Sanskrit in the 10th Century AD has a mention of a brew called 'Shama pani', the decoction of 'shamapatra', meaning the leaves. The word 'cha' must have been derived from 'shama' which found its way to China, they aruge. According to *Nidana*, Shamapani

*Sanskrit scholars are of the opinion that Sanjeevani plant which finds expression in Ramayana may well be tea!*

was used as a medicine against cold, cough, headache and drowsiness.

Mont Fort Chamney says, "The tea plant in not indigenous of China and the seed from which it was first grown there is traditionally said to have been brought to China from Assam". Another tea authority Samuel Ball notes. "There are reasons to believe that the tea plant was transported from China to Assam in pre-historic days". Yet another tea researcher observed, after extensive touring in the South and Indo China region, that the China tea was of a distinctive variety when compared to that of Assam and Cambodia. Hence, he postulated that the primary origin of tea might have been located in the Arctic circle or even the Mongolian plateau!

But the most common consensus is that the fan shaped area between China, Northeast India and Myanmar was the place from where tea originated and then spread to other parts of the world.

*Young tea plant with flower.*

# The Tea Family

Tea belongs to the family Camellieaceae (which has 30 genera and 500 species). The genera Cammellia includes 82 species. Three main jats are the Assam variety called *Cassmica*, the China variety known as *C-sinensis* and the hybrid termed *C.assamica Sp lasiocalyx.*

During early years there was confusion regarding nomenclature of tea which was termed *Thea Sinensis* in 1753, later *Thea Viridis* (viridis meaning green tea) and *Thea Bohea* (referring to black tea). When the Assam variety was discovered it was *Thea Assamica*. A full stop to this confusion was arrived at in the International Botanical Congress in 1935 at Amsterdam, when it was decided that tea would go by the name *C.sinensis*.

Generic name Camellia was derived from George Joseph Kamel or Camellus (1661–1706), Moravina Jesuit who wrote about the plants of Asia. And Sinensis indicates China. Technically, the correct botanical name is Camellia Sinensis (L) O.Kuntze, which includes the authority who gave it its final shape. Today pure breeds are rare due to cross pollination over centuries.

The word 'tea' was derived from T'e in Fukien dialect and 'cha' from Cantanese dialect of China. Tea is actually a tree, which, if left to grow, will reach 12 to 15 meters height with exceedingly sturdy stem and deep taproot. It is believed that in China monkeys were used to gather tea leaves. And the early pluckers of India rode on elephants!

*The early pluckers of India rode on elephants*

# Tea and China

Whatever be the speculations about the origin of tea, it is widely believed that planned commercial cultivation of tea began in China. Starting with simple hand rolling, the Chinese brought about revolutionary changes in tea manufacture and methods of brewing.

Tea became a common medicinal drink during the Han dynasty (206 BC to 221 AD). During the 5th century AD, tea became an article of trade in China. Popularity of tea reached newer heights during the Tang period (618–906 AD), which emancipated tea from its crude state and led to its final idealisation. The first tea tax was imposed in 783 AD.

Ch'a Ching or Tea Classic was written in 780 AD by the greatest Tea Maker Lu Yu when he was commissioned by the Chinese tea merchants to write a comprehensive book on the subject. Even today, Ch'a Ching is considered an Encyclopedia on tea and "a tea tipplers bible", which gave tremendous impetus to Chinese tea trade. Thus Lu Yu is acclaimed to be the "Apostle of tea" and "the patron saint of the Chinese tea merchants", who framed strict rules and wrote about the spiritual enjoyment of the brew rather than physical satisfaction. According to him, "for exquisite freshness and vibrant fragrance, limit the number of cups of three. If one can be satisfied with less than perfection, five are permissible!"

Tea rituals were performed in Buddhist temples as far back as the Tang period, when brick tea was ceremoniously pared, hot water added and ladled into ceramic bowls, offered to the deity by the monks who sat in solemn silence in front of the image of Bodhidharma and drank tea out of a single bowl. Lu Yu had even laid down the conversation proper to the tea room, the etiquette to be observed and the ideal atmosphere that was conducive to the ceremony, which was performed with tea quipage comprising 24 articles as prescribed in Ch'a Ching.

Only during the Sung Dynasty (600–1280 AD) tea was admired even by the common man and tea houses sprang up everywhere. Households began to have special tea rooms for preparing and drinking the brew and entertaining guests.

Obsession with tea reached such heights that Li Chi Lai, a Taoist poet of the Sung Dynasty held that there were three deplorable acts in the world i.e...., the spoiling of youth through false education, the degradation of fine paintings through vulgar admiration and the wasting of fine tea through improper manipulation!

There was a decline in tea drinking habits in China due to invasion of the Mongol tribes during the 13th century. It was revived during the reign of Yuen dynasty (1280–1368 AD) and the native Ming dynasty (1368–1644 AD). People started believing that tea enabled a dead person to attain heaven so it was widely used in the worship of the dead with daily offerings to their forebears. This custom still prevails even today among ethnic Chinese expatriates outside the Communist mainland. It is said that during the Ming period it was experimented to produce varieties of greens, blacks and oolongs.

Even though China concealed the secret of tea drinking for thousands of years, its spread across the borders and off shore of China was a natural phenomenon to follow because of trade and religio-cultural exchanges. Travel accounts of traders and aristocrats reveal the tea habits of different countries in the past.

*Tea garden in China.*

## Tea in India

The story of tea in India dates back to 1774 when the first shipment of tea seeds was imported from China for planting in the Botanical Garden at Kolkata, when Lord Warren Hastings as the Governor General of India. In 1778, at the behest of the Company, Sir Banks, Director of the Royal Botanical Garden at Kew prepared a report on the possibilities of cultivating new crops in the Colony in which he termed tea as "an article of the greatest national importance" to Britain and favourably recommended its cultivation. In 1793, Sir Banks was sent to China to acquire detailed knowledge of tea cultivation and manufacture.

In 1815, Col. Latter reported on the drinking habit of Assam tribes. Robert Bruce, a one time employee of East India Company also learnt about Assam tea from an Assamese nobleman named Maniram Dutta Barua who facilitated the Scot's friendship with the Singpho Chief, Beesa Gam. Thus Bruce struck a deal with the Chief for supply of tea seeds and plants. But he died in 1824. However, his younger brother Charles Alexander Bruce contacted Maniram in 1825 for the same trade purpose. On February 26, 1826 through Yandaboo Treaty the British annexed the territory of Kamarupa, (the old name for Assam) "to turn Assam into one agricultural estate of tea drinking Britons."

By 1833 tea import from China was almost endangered due to hostilities between the Chinese and the British, when the latter started trading opium instead of silver in the barter deal for tea with the former. This resulted in the Opium wars. Hence in 1834, Lord Bentinck formed the historic Tea Committee to explore all avenues for tea cultivation in India. As a response to the Committee's circular, Captain. E. Jenkins, the Agent to the Governor General for the North East Frontier recommended Assam as ideal for tea planting. His tea collections were sent to the Tea Committee, which then recommended that the Assam tea jat "under proper management could be cultivated with complete success for commercial purposes."

In 1835, a Scientific Commission, comprising Dr Wallich, Dr W. Griffith and Dr J. Mc.Lelland, was appointed by the Tea committee to select suitable sites for setting up the Indian Tea Industry with the help of C. A. Bruce. After discussions and disputes, it was decided that the China plant be used instead of Assam tea. Seeds were imported from China. And the first tea plantation, set up on Kunadlimukh, Sadiya at the char—a temporary sand bank created by a

*The historic planter's club – The High Range Club.*

shifting river—turned out to be a failure since by the following monsoon the new plantation was flooded and flushed away by the rain waters!

C.A. Bruce, who by then held the post of Superintendent of Tea Culture in Assam, shifted the salvaged plants from the Kundalimukh to Jaipur, some of which are said to be surviving even today. In 1837 some of these plants were used to began Chabuwa (Chaboa in Assamese means tea planting) Plantations.

By this time, Chinese plants with local variety hybrids were produced in the Botanical Garden at Calcutta. They were

*Young tea clearing brought into plucking.*

sent to Dehradun, Kumaon, Garhwal and Kangra in North India and Nilgiris and Wyanad in the South.

In 1836 Bruce successfully dispatched a small sample of manufactured tea out of the harvest from wild tea bushes, which he grew in his nurseries with the help of the Singphos in Assam, to England. The samples were sent to the Viceroy Lord Auckland who certified it as good tea. By December the same year the London Produce market recorded the receipt of one pound of Indian Tea which increased to five pounds the following year. By May 1838, 350 pounds of Assam tea, mainly from the native Assam jat arrived at London. The tea tasters in London described the samples as "tea, good, middling, strong, high burnt, rather smoky, Pekoe kind, and if there was any deficiency in its character it arose from want of care in preparation, rather than from the quality of the plant."

Tea dispatches from India over the years increased by leaps and bounds. In 1838 some merchants in Calcutta at the behest of the Company formed the Bengal Tea Association (BTA). In 1839, Assam came under the direct administration of the British, which gave further fillip to private tea enterprises. The same year a joint stock company was formed in London, which along with the BTA was merged

*A tea field under plucking.*

and the first Indian Tea Company called Assam Company was formed. The first tea auction in London was held on January 10, 1839.

In the following years, the tea industry faced a lot of hardships in the form of pestilence and labour problems so much so that it was on the verge of collapse. But in 1847 the turning point came. The management was tightened up and the methods of cultivation and manufacture were improved under the stewardship of Henry Burkin Young and Stephen Mornay. In five years time the tea industry again became a success story.

Private parties came into the scene following Lt. Col. F.S. Hannay, the first European proprietorial tea planter in 1851.

The Williamson Brothers acquired large tracts of land for setting up plantations. They were the ones who had completely done away with the Chinese bush, which assumed historical significance.

In 1859, a second tea company, Jorhaut Tea Company was formed. That year saw the birth of 51 tea gardens in Assam. The Tea Planters Association was formed the same year to bring outside labour through their agents to streamline systematic and organised recruitment. In 1861, Lord Canning framed new laws, which permitted 'white entrepreneurs' to purchase land through auction. This resulted in a mad rush for acquisition of land. The same year saw the birth of the Calcutta Auction Center. In 1862, there were 120 plantations owned by 51 private individuals or companies and 5 public companies.

The 'Tea Mania' in the 1860s had negative effects as well. The mad purchase of tea tracts for very high costs led to lots of socio-economic problems. Some could not manage the property and sold them for cheap prices. Many became bankrupt and indebted, and some even committed suicide.

A commission of Enquiry was set up in 1868 to investigate into the maladies of the tragedy for fruitful remedies. Various other Inquiry Committees & Commissions had to be formed

*An old tea field under plucking.*

and even legislations passed by the Government to mitigate the problem of labour and for the amelioration of the plantation workers in the North. By 1870s the industry blew over the crisis. It started thriving again with improved quantity and quality. In 1872 new tea gardens were opened.

Only during this time the pattern of garden management had taken shape. And only by 1940s, Indian Assistantance came into the plantation picture. George M. Baker, an Assam planter belonging to the second breed after the pioneer planters, said in 1884: "A manager of a tea garden must be rather out of the ordinary sort of man. To be of any use, he must be of strict integrity, in order to gain the confidence of his employees; sober, business like, a good accountant, not easily ruffled, handy at carpenteering and engineering and have a smattering of information on all subjects; or, to put it concisely, he must be a veritable jack of all trades!"

In South India, Dr Christie experimented with tea as early as in 1832 and experimental planting of saplings brought from Calcutta's Botanical Gardens were thriving by the year 1839. But commercial planting began here only from 1859 in Nilgiris in Tamil Nadu, Central Travancore in 1875, Kanan Devan Hills in 1878, Wyanad in 1889 and Anamallais in 1897. UPASI was established in 1983 and its Scientific Department in 1903. The Tocklai Experimental Station was opened in 1912. The Indian Tea Cess Act was passed in 1902 to raise funds to defray the expenditure necessary for tea propaganda abroad. In 1944 excise duty on tea was levied for the first time.

Today India is the largest tea producer in the world followed by China and Sri Lanka. India's total tea area is about 5,00,000 hectares with a production of more than 870 million Kgs. The industry employs more than 10,00,000 people. Indian tea is exported to 80 countries and accounts for about 15% of the world tea trade.

## *The Global Flow*

The first country to learn of tea from China is Tibet, whose favourite national drink is yak buttered tea. It is said that a Tibetan drinks 30 to 50 cups of tea a day! And one of his favourite meals is "Tjampa", a dish prepared with ingredients such as powdered rice or beans made into a paste with yak-buttered tea.

The Mongolians added salt and animal tallow to boiling brick tea (ages ago tea was made in cake or brick form, before the powdered form came into vogue) and strained and mixed with milk, butter and roasted meal and this mixtures was fortified diet for the Mongolians, a means to survive in the biting cold.

In Myanmar, a vegetable relish called "Letpet" is prepared out of tea plants. For preparing letpet, tea leaves are first boiled, stuffed into bamboo and buried for several months for fermentation. The resuscitated leaves are then sliced into a salad form by mixing oil, garlic, fried shrimps, fruits, dried coconut etc. Letpet steeped in oil is served to the newly weds in Myanmar, for it is believed that it will ensure conjugal bliss!

The Shan tribe of northern Thailand steam or boil the tea leaves which then are laced with salt, garlic, dried fish, pork etc. to be chewed or eaten. Then Bhutanese prepare a compound of water, flour, butter, salt and Bohea tea with some other ingredients; boil it, beat it up and intimately blend together to enjoy the drink. Trade routes carried tea to Middle East countries as far as Persia (Iran) where fennel, cloves and sugar were added to tea.

*Japanese Tea ceremony.*

Tea came into in Japan around 593 AD, brought by the Buddhist monks. However, the first instance of tea planting is believed to have commenced in the 8th century AD when an Emperor called Shomu (729 AD) gave tea plants as gift. A Buddhist monk named Gyoki was reputed to have built forty-nine temples in Japan—in each of which he planted tea. During Emperor Saga's regime, it was decreed that tea be planted for royal consumption and drunk in royal banquets. Tea being an integral part of Zen rituals, it flourished in Japan when the military class called Samurai gained political prominence in the 12th century and arduously promoted Zen philosophy.

*Traditional method of serving tea in Japan.*

The tea room in Japan symbolises the oriental belief that tea is the "exlixir of immortality" and "the nectar fit for the gods". The tea room should perfectly reflect the very aim of tea ceremony. It is said that "not a colour to distinct the tone of the room, not a sound to mar the rhythm of things, not a gesture to uptrude the harmony, not a word to break the unity of the surroundings and all movements to be performed simply and naturally".

With the passage of time, tea began to be identified with Japanese culture and tea drinking became more and more popular. By the time the Europeans found their way to the Far-East in the 16th century it is said that tea drinking in Japan and China had reached the epitome of refinement. Today it is said that the tea ceremony has become a commercialised showpiece rather than an art of living and worship of good taste and refinement, as it used to be.

After the historic sea route exploration by Vasco da Gama in the 15th century, the aroma of tea started attracting the Europeans. In the early part and in the middle of the 16th century the Chinese and Japanese shores were opened to the Europeans and the Jesuit missionaries

*Vasco da Gama.*

and the explorers were the first Europeans to taste "the bitter red medicinal beverage of China".

Even though the Portuguese were the first to enjoy tea and take back some to Europe, they did not embark upon full-scale trading. It was the enterprising Dutch who effected the earliest transportation of tea in 1607 and sold it to the aristocracy and upper middle class of Europe for a high price. Tea at once became a status symbol of the elite, who relished "the exquisite froth of the liquid Jade" in lavish tea parties.

By 1653, tea became a fashionable drink in the Dutch Court. Imports increased, cost went down. Ounce packs were introduced and sold by apothecaries. The oriental drink started permeating to middle and lower classes too.

In the following two decades Netherlands was transformed into the first tea-drinking nation in Europe. By 1680 it is said that every tea smitten lady in Holland had a tea room in her house and started holding regular tea parties which resulted in neglecting of domestic duties and consequently to furious husbands!

Within five decades of its introduction to Europe, tea started flowing abundantly into every other country of the continent. The French took to tea instantly when the Dutch introduced it in around 1636. Tea salons mushroomed in Paris by 1648 and Germany followed suit. The credit for adding milk to tea goes to the French.

*Tea drinking in Europe.*

Tea entered England around 1652–54. The first sale in London was held in 1657 and in 1668, 134 pounds of tea was imported from Java. 1669 onwards the East Indian Company continued to ship teas from Java to Madras and from there in Company ships to England. From 1689 onwards, direct shipments to London were chartered. The epidemic madness of importing tea into Europe from China was vehemently condemned by many.

Tea started to receive royal patronage from 1666 when the East India Company presented the Queen with a large quantity of tea. A cask of cold tea was a valued present those days since tea enjoyed the status of an aristocratic drink and was out of reach of the common man.

*Tea enjoyed the status of an aristocratic drink.*

Only by the second decade of 18th century tea no longer remained confined only to elite circles due to availability of cheaper varieties. Tea was available everywhere—from pharmacy to grocery. There was a phenomenal rise in tea imports to the country. This shifted the scene—rich and the refined of the high society stopped going to coffee houses and preferred what came to be known as exclusive tea houses and tea gardens. Slowly the ladies also were granted the privilege to enter the teahouses, which were initially meant for only men.

In 1830s in England when the poor sections of industrial workers were in the habit of drowning their worries in alcohol, the Temperance Movement Reformers offered tea as an alternative and consequently elaborate Tea meetings were held to discuss the sorrowful plight of industrial workers.

Notwithstanding the growing popularity of tea in England there was also stiff resistance from some quarters. There were vociferous demands that the Government should ban tea altogether! The tea traders were even compared to drug peddlers! John Wesly, the founder of Methodist Church denunciated tea in 1748 after complaining 'symptoms of a paralytic disorder with nerves all unstrung, bodily strength quite decayed!' He went a step further and formed a sort of de-addiction camp with other tea addicts! Another English man William Cobbet, a writer and politician, criticised the nation for wasting its time and energy on tea. Jonnan Hanvey in an essay on tea came out with a seething attack on tea by calling it a beverage "pernicious to health, obstructing industry and impoverishing the nation".

When this was the case with the learned men, the Ayrshire farmers also started raising their dissenting voices by signing an anti-tea pledge and terming tea as "that foreign and consumptive luxury". They preferred to leave the enjoyment of it altogether to those "who can afford to be weak, indolent and useless!"

But European intellectuals, writers, artists and philosophers appreciated the value of this beverage not as a temporary fascination but as a wonder drink that gave an 'eternity of pleasure' and urged the 'tranquility of the soul'. They disregarded the tea antagonists' prejudicial criticisms which, they thought, mainly sprang from the indigestible fact that tea is basically an oriental drink and not so intoxicating as beer or for that matter coffee, which give more kick than tea!

Literary giants like Lord Byron, Dr. Samuel Johnson, John Ruskin, Coleridge, Charles Lamb, Shelley, John Keats, W.M.

Thackery, and H.W. Long Fellow drank tea as a stimulant for their imagination. In fact, John Ruskin was not only an avowed tea drinker himself but also opened a shop to sell low priced tea to the poor, which had to be shut down because "the poor only wish to buy tea where it is brightly lit and eloquently ticketed".

As years rolled by, the thirst for the brew increased further and Britain became a tea-guzzling nation. 1820 marked the end of an era and the beginning of another. China's hegemony in tea trade was dealt with a severe blow by the British entering in it in full swing by establishing a tea empire! In 1887 for the first time, British imports from her gardens in India and Ceylon exceeded imports from China.

*Tea plucking in Sri Lanka.*

17th century was a milestone in spread of tea across the nations. The first tea arrival record in Russia dates back to 1618, which was a gift from the Chinese Ambassador to the Czar. By 1689 Russia became a giant importer of tea from China and by 18th century Russia turned to be a tea-drinking nation. Even today Russia figures in the tea map quite prominently despite the disintegration of the erstwhile USSR.

# Boston Tea Party

It was the Dutch, who took tea to USA around 1650 and by the later half of the 17th century, tea became a popular beverage in America. The over-ambitious East India Company naturally tried to wrest the tea monopoly from the Dutch and eventually took total control of the colonial tea trade in the US. Heavy duties in the form of excise and revenue were imposed on tea and several other acts were passed by the British government, during King George III's rule, under the compulsion of the company.

Nonetheless the Dutch smuggled tea into US and sold it for cheaper rates. As a counter attack the British parliament through its Tea Act in 1773 authorised the East India Company to import tea directly to US, doing away with middle men and thus cutting down the tea prices. But the Americans, whose patriotic ire had already been roused due to the three-pence-for-a-pound-of-tea duty, didn't take the forceful trade intrusion and legal restrictions meekly.

On the fateful day, on 16 December 1773, three ships of the East India Company carrying their tea cargo, unaware of the awaiting danger at the Boston harbour, dropped anchors. Various organisations calling themselves as Sons of Liberty held protest demonstrations against British ships. That same day, a gang of men disguised as Mohawk Red Indians, led by Samuel Adams boarded the ships and threw away 342 chests of tea into the sea. That historic event is the Boston Tea Party, which heralded the birth of a new nation called America. It is said the several other such 'tea parties' in Philadelphia, Greenwich and Charleston followed the Boston Tea Party.

The Americans often shocked the orthodox tea drinkers with their fancy flavours like orange, apricot, pineapple, peppermint etc. In some cases, popular American "Mixes" contains just 3% of instant tea!

Like the flavoured tea, U.S.A. is also considered to be the birthplace of the tea bags. The concept of tea bag was developed from an innovative marketing idea of a New York dealer called Thomas Sullivan in 1908 who sold tea for the first time in hand sewn silk bags to his customers. This bag was not meant for brewing but some over enthusiastic customers must have brewed the bag itself with tea in it and they criticised the use of silk for making such bags! Sullivan then changed to more cheaper gauze material and thought 'why not?' The tea bag was born and by 1920 it was an established practice. Now perforated paper is used as tea bag and the one with a string and a bag is meant for cup brewing and the stringless is for pots.

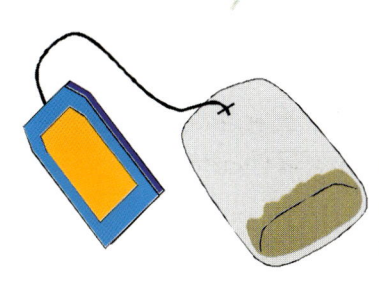

The tea bags have their own advantages and disadvantages. The advantage being, in traditional brewing we can make 485 cups per kilo, whereas in the case of tea bags

320 cups can be made (in some countries like South Africa 400 bags) using one kg tea and each tea bag producing two cups, thereby 640 cups in total (or 800 cups in the case of South African bags). The disadvantage is that because of the less quantity of tea packed in the bags there came a decline in the tea export scenario. That is to say that the countries which preferred tea bags started importing lesser quantity of tea as the consumption level fell.

# *Changing Trends*

*One year old tea clonal plant ready for planting.*

The present day tea-culture techniques emerged over centuries through a process of trial and error. Scattering seeds was the first method of sowing/planting. The seed-at-stake method followed, in which shallow holes were dug with uniform spacing and seeds planted. Tea nursery

*Tea Nursery*

concept evolved to select the best uniforms saplings. Later seeds barries (gardens) were set up to overcome the drawback of poly clonals. Controlled cross-pollination enabled biclonal seeds that were hardier and better. The Tocklai Tea Experimental Station, the oldest Tea Research Centre in the world, introduced vegetative propagation or clonal planting, which ensured uniformity of bushes and was greatly preferred. Still seeds are very much required to secure better hybrids. Tissue culture followed, for developing higher yielding, disease resistant strains of tea. This method is yet to take off in a large scale.

Cultural practices like plucking, pruning, manuring etc. have also undergone a sea change in the past based on research. The style, cycle and height of pruning has changed. Dr. Eden says, "Pruning is still more of an art than a science, because the physiology of the tea bush is still very imperfectly understood… There is no single aspect of tea cultivation that is so controversial as that of pruning!"

By 1920s inorganic manures replaced organic manures. And today it seems that the wheel has gone a full circle as there is a great demand for organic tea in the global market. It is

*Tea plucking – the mainstay operation in a tea plantation.*

*Garden fresh tea leaves moving through conveyors over the withering troughs in a tea factory.*

said that even though the focus is on organic farming, tea plantations can not do away with inorganic fertilizers, insecticides, and weedicides due to various factors like cost, time, enormity of operational area etc. Also, it is established that the end product does not contain traces of pesticides or weedicides, which makes tea safe for drinking. Today there are potential bio-control agents for pest and even weed control.

Plucking—the delicate and prime operation is said to have evolved as early as 1870s. Formerly, the whole young shoots were also plucked and no initial growth was allowed. It was George Williamson Senior, a tea planter in Assam who brought about the major change in the practice allowing the saplings to grow for a couple of years before plucking. Two or three leaves and a bud is the accepted pattern throughout the world. And bud plucking is practised to get the finest tea. G.M. Baker remarks, "The process of plucking is not nearly so easy as it looks; the plant requires delicate handling and the knack takes some time to acquire, the difference between an old hand and a beginner is transparent in the quantity and quality of leaf brought to scale".

Specially designed shears with bag attachment were in widespread use in Japan between the World Wars. Slowly mechanisation of field operations started. Today countries

*The process of withering tea leaves in a factory.*

like Russia, Kenya and Uganda are using heavy weight giant machines for tea harvesting, which not only use cutters but also conveyors and leaf hoppers. It is said that in Mauritius, Japanese Kawasaki machines harvest 500 kgs of tea a day within four and half hours! However mechanisation can never replace human operation in plantation.

The metamorphosis of tea from plucking table to dining table is also an interesting story and is the result of continuous research. From batch process of those days, manufacturing has become a continuous conveyor belt process.

James Nelson, a planter of Cachar in Assam, seeing the long and laborious process of hand rolling tea by workers standing around long rectangular tables, one fine day got a

*A CTC Roller in action.*

brilliant idea. Why not invert a table of another and do the crushing and rolling? He instructed his workers to try the idea. It worked! He improved the version with his cut drill trousers forming a bag for the tea leaves. Nelson Tea Roller was invented!

In 1860s, Rolling Tables were patented by the British in India. In 1931 CTC (Crush, Tear and Curl) machine was invented by William Mckercher, Chairman of Amgoorie Tea Estate which revolutionised black tea manufacture. CTC's rival LTD (Lawrie Tea Processor) which pulverises the leaf was also invented. In 1950 came the Rotorvane invented by Ian Mc Tair.

Tea leaves are plucked, weighed, transported, weighed again, withered for physical change (removing moisture to make the leaf flaccid and rubbery to make it suitable for crushing and rolling) and chemical changes (to lose $Co_2$ and to break down protein into essential aminoacids) for 12-16 hours, rolled (to rupture leaf cells and release enzymes and to tear and curl the leaf), fermented (for oxidation and condensation of tea catechins) fired, graded and packed. Whole leaf, broken, fannings and dust (orthodox) broken fannings and dust (CTC) are the kinds of tea with a whole range of grades under each like FP, BOP, BOPF and SFD.

# Varieteas

The prepared tea comes in different forms: the fermented black tea, the unfermented green tea and partially fermented oolong tea (Ou-long meaning dragon). Pouchang is a scented variety tea in Taiwan where before the last firing, tea is scented with flowers such as gardinia and jasmine. Today speciality blends like Darjeeling, Uva Cyclon, Formosa Oolong also adorn the tea shelves.

Towards the end of World War II the king of convenience teas, instant tea, was produced by a method combining extraction of water-soluble solids, and conversion of the same into a powdery form by spray drying method. This could be from black tea as is done in USA or from green tea as patented by Tocklai Tea Experimental Station of Assam. The instant tea can be packed in concentrated powder form or as granules or even as tea pills! There are two types of instant tea—hot water-soluble and cold water soluble. From the appropriate type, products like tea cola, packed tea, liquid and frozen concentrate can be made.

A huge variety of tea preparations are savoured today. Tea is drunk now cold or hot not only with lemon, but cherries, strawberries and even a dash of rum! High balls or cocktails with tea are made by mixing soda, fruit juices or ginger. with the brew. Tea punches and tea ice creams are known tea recipes. An enterprising Sri Lankan prepared tea cider by allowing the extract to ferment for 2 to 3 days and then

*A huge variety of tea preparations are savoured today.*

distilling it. If the fermentation process is allowed to continue for a month, what we will get is tea vinegar!

Drinking tea a worldwide habit. Different traditional rituals are associated with tea drinking. For Indians generally, tea drinking is a part of their lives. They drink tea at different times, in the morning, as an afternoon stimulant, as a relaxant after a hard day's work and for a feeling of togetherness shared with a loved one!

*A feeling of togetherness shared with a loved one.*

# Tea Consumption in India

The highest per capita tea consumption in India is in Jammu & Kashmir according to a study made by Prof. V.N. Reddy and Prof. Amitava Bose. The per capita consumption there is 1594 grams. Punjab with 1525 grams comes second. The consumption pattern is as follows: Gujarat 1222 grams, Kerala 1100 grams, UP 376 grams, Tamil Nadu 366 grams, Orissa 276 grams, Bihar 232 grams, Maharashtra 1000 grams, West Bengal 464 grams, Madhya Pradesh 618 grams,

Rajasthan 818 grams, Karnataka 750 grams, Harayana 1026 grams and Assam 714 grams.

The largest quantity of tea is consumed in Maharashtra with 83 million kgs per annum. This forms 15 per cent of the total domestic consumption in India. Uttar Pradesh with 56 million kilos is in the second position. The lowest consumption is in Orissa with 9 million kgs.

People of West Bengal and Orissa drink CTC broken teas. At the same time, the CTC dust is popular in shops and restaurants. People in Bihar like CTC Dust Tea. Majority of North Indians drink CTC broken tea. Rajasthanis are fond of CTC Fannings. People of Central India also like CTC Dust Tea.

Of all the three non-intoxicating hot beverages in the world, tea is the most popular beverage. (The other two are coffee and cocoa). Tea has become synonymous not

*A popular brand of tea.*

only with civilised behaviour, decorous conversation and graceful hospitality but also with good health. The traditional belief that tea is a healthy drink, is today backed by science which has proved tea's nutritive and therapeutic values beyond dispute. And hence drinking tea without any admixture is acclaimed as the best way to benefit from the wonder drink.

Half the population on earth drinks tea and over 800 million cups of tea is consumed everyday! The world's per capita consumption is soaring year after year and demand for tea is forever on the rise!

# Tea Plantations and Environment

There are two major accusations against tea plantations: Large-scale conversions of forest lands into plantations during the pioneering days of the European planters and the use of pesticides and chemical fertilizers detrimental to the environment.

As regards the first accusation, from the mid 19th century to the early part of the last century when the tea plantations were raised there was neither a legal regulation in the country for environment conservation nor eco-awareness among the planters for protecting the forests.

In fact, in some tea plantation areas, such as the one in the High Range of Kerala there are large tracts of shoals which have been actually preserved by the planters. The main reasons were species protection, water conservation, provision of wildlife corridor and wind damage control.

In the 1950s the Kanan Devan Hills Produce Company in Munnar (Kerala) wanted to clear the Mankulam forest areas, which was a part of its plantation area, to establish cardamom plantations. The Munnar regional office sought permission from the company headquarters in London. The office sought clarification on two aspects: whether it would affect the rainfall pattern and threaten the elephant habitat. When

*Yellow Pansy.*

*Wild life near tea plantation.*

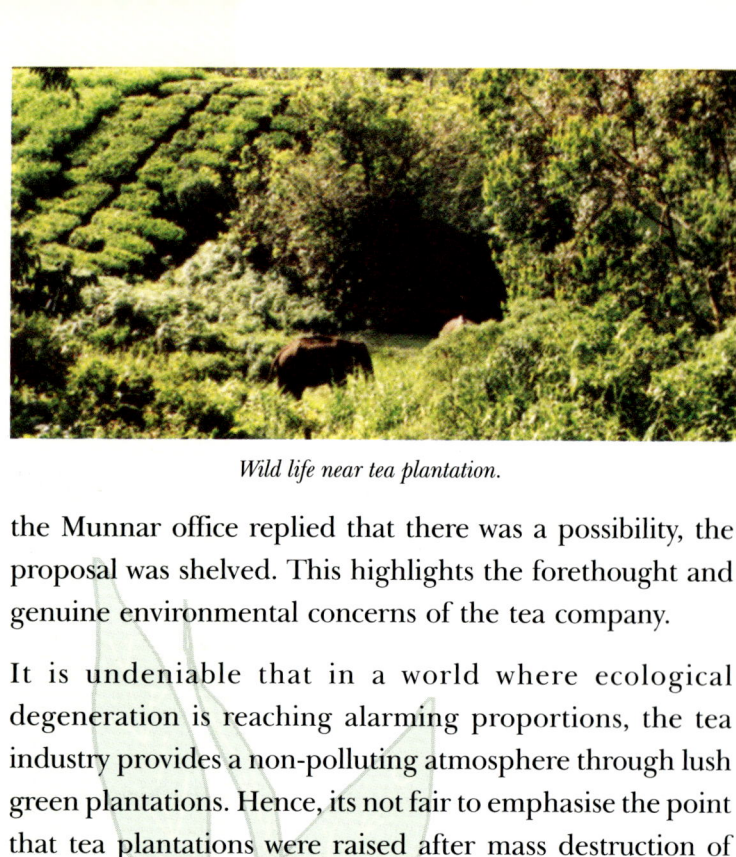

the Munnar office replied that there was a possibility, the proposal was shelved. This highlights the forethought and genuine environmental concerns of the tea company.

It is undeniable that in a world where ecological degeneration is reaching alarming proportions, the tea industry provides a non-polluting atmosphere through lush green plantations. Hence, its not fair to emphasise the point that tea plantations were raised after mass destruction of forests.

As we all known, raising tea plantations was one of the major economic activities during the colonial rule in India. Today, the tea industry is one of the largest foreign exchange earners for India. And the tea industry is one of the well-organised industries in the world, providing employment to millions of people directly or indirectly.

For example, the Indian Tea industry employs over 1.1 million workers directly, the largest in any industry. It looks after more than 5 million dependant of employees and supports more than 50,000 small tea growers. Of the working population directly employed by the tea industry, half are women.

*A hospital in a tea garden.*

As regards the second point, it must be mentioned that the tea plantations use only agro-chemicals that have been approved by the Central Insecticides Board of India and the Environmental Protection Agency of the USA.

These chemicals, further tested and certified by the Tea Scientific Department of the United Planters' Association of South India (UPASI) and the Tea Research Institute at Toklai, Assam, are used according to the recommended schedule and dosage. Fertilizer audits are also carried out to rationalise their use. In fact, leading tea plantations do not use the same chemical continuously but alternate them and keep the dosage to the bare minimum as the pesticide application is need based. Contrary to propaganda, the chemicals do not cause any environmental pollution. The final produce, tea, is also absolutely free of chemical residues.

Nevertheless, of late, tea plantations are slowly moving into organic tea production, realising its economic potential as well as its eco-friendliness.

*Feeding thermal energy for tea processing.*

The tea gardens had initiated steps long ago to convert the tea-waste into rich, useful organic manure by using the vermin-tech process. The services of the earthworm are utilised in a scientific manner to make green manure called the vermi-post. This helps reduce and replace the use of chemicals in the tea fields.

The tea industry does not depend on any chemical processing method in tea production. Neither any harmful effluent nor any liquid effluent is discharged from the tea factories. The tea industry meets the environmental standards and regulations with ease, unlike other industries.

Yet another commendable eco-conscious effort made by most tea plantations is the conservation of eco-equilibrium by keeping intact the tea plantations, fuel plantations, and shoals for more than half a century. By raising the fuel plantations, a major environmental hazard—burning of fossil fuels in the tea factories–is largely averted. Since the tea estates follow a rigid eight-year or ten-year cycle of felling only one-third of its own renewable energy plantations at a time, two thirds of the fuelwood corridor remain tall at any point of time.

# Let Legendary Tea Survive

The Indian tea industry has had its definite highs and lows, effecting it every four years so in a cyclical manner. And today the crisis faced by the industry seems to have reached an irredeemable stage, where the wheel of fortune lies battered and broken after many years of bumpy ride on rugged road of misfortune.

The tea crisis of course throws a lot of problems to the tea plantation companies and the government as well. But at the same time it challenges their ability for crisis management, the success of which lies in seeing clearly the possibility of riding the rough waves and reaching the shores with courage and conviction. It is time for the tea plantation industry to think out of the box. Quick innovation and implementation is the catchword.

When we talk about tea plantations, tea plantation tourism also comes to mind. It will serve two vital objectives. One is for studying and enjoying Mother Nature surrounding the tea plantations and the other is for knowing the plantation industry inside out. Tea plantations have a rich historical, archaeological, architectural, argo-climatic, geological, cultural, demographic and bio-diversity uniqueness.

The tea plantation tourism is a maiden venture, the possibilities of which have been least explored as far as India is concerned. Efforts should be made to develop tea plantation tourism package to overcome the crisis in the tea industry. Let the legendary tea survive for ever!

*Neela Kurinji (Strobilanthes kunthianus).*

## Tea Varieties

1. Black Tea - Black Tea is green tea leaf that is allowed to oxidize. It undergoes a fermentation process as part of production. Black tea has rich aroma and flavour and is one of the most popular teas in India.

2. Green Tea – A more healthy variety of tea of brownish-green colour. It has less aroma and flavour. Green tea is unfermented and is prepared by a process of steaming, processing and drying. Green tea is popular in China, Japan and Taiwan.

3. Oolong Tea – A semi-fermented, semi-oxidised tea produced mainly in the Fujian province of China and Taiwan. The trees grow up to as much as 90ft in height and hence monkeys pick the leaves. In India, organic Oolong tea is produced in Assam and Darjeeling.

4. Darjeeling Tea – Tea grown on the hill district of Darjeeling in India are also called 'Champagne Teas' because of their aroma resembling Muscat grapes. Mild in character; Darjeeling tea is popular throughout the world.

5. Nilgiri Tea – Tea grown in South India's Nilgiri Hills. It has a unique combination of fragrance and briskness.

6. Assam Tea – Tea grown in the plains of North East India – mostly CTC teas. It is strong and flavoury. Assam tea is blended with African tea or Ceylon tea to produce rich aroma and taste.

7. Sikkim Tea – A combination of Darjeeling's delicate flavours and light body and Assam's maltiness, this tea is grown in the state of Sikkim, India.

8. Ceylon Tea – One of the finest variety of tea. Rich flavour and bright golden colour, Ceylon tea is crisp and strong.

9. Keemun Tea (China) – Considered as an elite of Chinese Black Teas.

10. Lapsang Souchong Tea (China) – Is well known for its smoky taste.

11. Dooaras Tea – Tea from West Assam and West Bengal. Coloury with flavour-CTC, Orthodox and Green Tea.

12. Yunan Tea – An exotic tea from Yunan province in China which is considered to be the birthplace of tea cultivation.

# *Glossary*

Ayrshire: a place in Scotland
Bodhidharma: the Buddhist Monk who brought Zen Buddhism to China
BOP: Broken Orange Pekoe
BOPF: Broken Orange Pekoe Fannings
Cammellia Sinensis           }
Cammellia Sinensis Assamica  } All belongs to the tea family
Cammellia Cambodiensis}
Cammellia Sinensis: The common tea plant brought to China from India in the 4th century.
CTC: Crush, Tear and Curl
Czar: Ruler of Russia
Darjeeling Tea: Renowned for its aroma and flavor
FP: Flowery Pekoe
Han Dynasty: Ruler of China during 206 BC–220 AD
Kamarupa: Ancient name of Assam.
Lord William Bentinck: Governor General of India in 1833.
Lord Canning: First Viceroy of India.

Lord Warren Hastings: Governor General of India.

Lu Yu: Author of 'Book Of Tea' and 'Tea Classics' during the Tang Dynasty.

Lu You: A Chinese sage who wrote 'Tea Scriptures' during Sung Dynasty.

Meng Mountain: A world famous sacred mountain of China.

Ming Dynasty: Rulers of China during 1368–1644 AD.

Montford Chamney: Tea Planter and author of 'The Story of Tea Leaf.'

Orthodox: Making of black tea by withering, processing, oxidation and firing.

Pekoe: Derived from a Chinese world. Pekoe means that the leaves so graded were exclusively plucked from the tip of the branch: the leaf bud and the two leaves below the bud. In other words, the whole leaves were of uniform size.

Prof. V.N. Reddy and Prof. Amitava Bose: Professors at the Indian Institute of Management, Kolkatta.

SFD: Super Fine Dust

SRD: Super Red Dust

Sadiya: A place in present day Arunachal Pradesh which was part of Assam earlier.

Singpho and Khamti Tribes: Both were tribal people of Arunachal Pradesh.

Sir Joseph Banks: Director of the Royal Botanical Garden, Kew, London, was President of the Royal Society from 1778 to 1820.

Sung Dynasty: Rulers of China from 960–1270 AD.

Tang Dynasty: Rulers of China during 618–906 AD.

Temperance Movement: A major cause of Social reforms in Victoria Britain.

Tocklai Experimental Station: Tea research center in Assam.

UPASI: United Planters Association of South India.

Yandaboo Treaty: The treaty was to have perpetual peace and friendship between the East India Company and the King of Ava.

Yuen Dynasty: Chinese rulers during 1280–1368 AD

Zen: An East Asian form of Buddhism. This is practised primarily in Japan.

# Notes

# Notes